A Letterbox Across Time

A Letterbox Across Time

Bidyut Bhusan Jena

HAWAKAL

Published by Hawakal Publishers
185 Kali Temple Road, Nimta, Kolkata 700049
India

Email info@hawakal.com
Website www.hawakal.com

First edition: June 2020

Cover image: Shutterstock
Cover design: Bitan Chakraborty

ISBN: 978-81-945273-4-3

Price: 350 INR | USD 14.99

To the memory of

Dr. Muralidhar Das
Professor Tutun Mukherjee
Irrfan Khan

Acknowledgements

My sincere thanks to the team of Hawakal Publishers for publishing *A Letterbox Across Time*.

I am grateful to renowned poet, critic and translator K. Satchidanandan for launching and lauding my first book of poems – *Pages* (2019), and for reflecting upon my poetry for the blurb of this collection, which I'll cherish for ever.

I cannot thank Professor Don Adams of Florida Atlantic University enough for his empathetic reflection on my poetry for the blurb of this collection. One of the warmest human beings, his inimitable passion for Somerset Maugham was the point of instant connection between us.

I thank my friend, Nancy Isobel Anderson for her endearing write-up for the blurb of this collection and for being one of the passionate readers of my poetry. Nancy, I am looking forward to working with you.

I am beholden to Dr. Meenakshi Shivram for her valuable comments on the preface, which prompted me to look at it more objectively. Apart from being a noted translator, for which she has been awarded by the Central Sahitya Akademi, she is a charismatic teacher, a wonderful human being and someone in whose presence I discover my goodness.

I thank Dr. Amitendu Bhattacharya – poet, critic and translator, for suggesting me to send the manuscript to Hawakal Publishers. Thank you, Amit for the gift of friendship. You are an important part of my world. I am looking forward to seeing your poems in print.

One remembers therefore one is. I thank my friend Naba Deka – one of the passionate human beings and writers I know, for the gift of memory.

I am indebted to my family for everything.

Preface

Maybe a slight change in the grammar of its movement would have altered its destiny – now the leaf floated before me. I held it and released it to the ground in the hope of recreating the almost inaudible sound of its first fall. But I could not. The moment had eluded me by sliding surreptitiously into a wordless horizon. Maybe life thus enacts certain moments once and for all. Then, is life not a footnote to such a dimension – the elusive wordless realm? Is this then the realm of language – a region of the primal Word (*Shabda*)? As Raja Rao writes in his book, *The Meaning of India*, "If the transient speaks to the transient it becomes a cacophony. But if the eternal, the unchanging, speaks to the unchanging, in me, in you, we have one language." However, all one receives are words – not in their primal form, but in their orphaned, mundane, conflicting and interpretable variations. And all interpretations lead to conflict. In fact, one interprets therefore one is not.

We live in an ambience of interpretation by agreeing upon a certain web of words and their meanings. This web is used and reused with the hope of making this quotidian existence a bit more convenient. In a way, it lends a sense of security to our existence – a domain of repetition. And, we, the creatures of novelty, from time to time, reject the consolation of repetition. If we do not, life will be easier. We reject repetition, because, unlike other animals (most likely) that are driven by necessity alone, we seek. In fact, this is one of the reasons why we are called *mortals* – a Greek word for humans, for it is only humans that know that they will die. Though they do not fully grasp what it is to die, they do not cease to meditate upon it (however the Indic Traditions, Buddhism in particular, believes that the elephant is the only animal that remembers all its previous births). Maybe it is this heightened awareness of impermanence, which turns them into seekers. And this exploration somehow makes them ruthlessly realign the notion of time – human time or historical time.

Poets are a strange tribe in this regard. They live through the season of decay – a timeless existence in a temporal script. Thus poetry, forever, veers into the original territory of time and towards its primitive essence – the *anahata* (unhurt or the unstruck sound). The words in poetry are unhurt, because they are incessantly in search of their original meanings – a primeval coexistence of the eternal principles of Prkrti and Purusa (as in Samkhya Darshana). Here we are reminded of the great Kavi (the poet as sage) Kalidasa's *Raghuvamsa*, "Vagarthaviva sampriktau vagarthah pratipattaye/Jagatah pitarau vande parvathiparameshwarau"[1]. Unlike the mundane life of words in our day-to-day transaction, poetry does not exist in human time or historical time alone. It belongs to the same orbit as Being, Eternity and the Word as silence and light (the original Word as the World – Bhartrhari's *Vakyapadiya*[2]). Therefore, like the Word, Poetry is in and with time, but not of time (thus the word *Sahitya*[3]). Thus it is eternal. And it is the life's work of the Kavi to take us back to the Original Word, when it existed with its corresponding meaning. As Raja Rao posits, "The word seems to come first as an impulsion from the nowhere, and then as a prehension, and it becomes less and less esoteric – till it begins to be concrete. And the concrete becoming ever more earthy, and the earthy communicated, as the common word, alas, seems to possess least of that original light. The writer or the poet is he who seeks back the common word to its origin of silence, that the manifested word become light." (*The Meaning of India*)

Therefore, the Kavi has the mission of sanctifying and further enabling the words to regain their primal meaning, thereby paving the way to a common language (here we are reminded of Paul Celan – a champion of German neologisms, he strove to unburden the German language of the unethical cargo it had acquired during the war by sanctifying and freeing it from the morass of lies and hatred). After carrying the burden of meanings that do not belong to them for long, words (the Word) crave for healing through a magical touch; very much like that of Rama's. Is Ahalya then the misunderstood Word? Is Rama the Kavi? Maybe George Steiner's observation[4] that human beings create language as they have an intrinsic urge to hide can be put to rest if the common language is discovered or the primal meaning of words restored. Maybe to some extent imagery plays an important role in this regard, by creating universal pictures of various emotional states. Thus imagery is an attempt at that universal language. However, it cannot be denied that certain images are culture-specific and there is a danger in trying to universalize them. In this context the role of translation (*rupantar* or *anuvad*) becomes important as an attempt at either universalising meaning or creating newer modes of understanding through the transference of shades of experience.

Since the poet is preoccupied with the mission of discovering the primal or universal language, his utterance must be free from the burden of binaries. His vision must be non-dual or advaitic. If his perception is biased, then the intended destination would forever remain an unattainable elsewhere. Therefore, the weeding out of any kind of dualized dimension in poetry presupposes an intrinsic freedom from the trammels of thought-slavery. It is my contention that poets should not be a slave to any ideology. They should learn the art of standing proudly outside the dualized (and sometimes myopic) ghettos of ideology. However, they must have a vision, which from time-to-time is realigned to meet the shifting shades of existence. It is possible that in this process they might tilt to different ideas and systems of thought from time to time. But they should not stagnate at any goalpost. Their vision should be so vast that the entire cosmos could be encapsulated in it, thereby turning their creation into an extension of the world of which they a part. But they must continue to remain impoverished or unfulfilled in some way or the other, for worldly fulfilment has the potential to nip the very being of art in the bud. They need an immeasurable emptiness within to hear the echoes of their being. Maybe it is this emptiness that the Swedish poet, Par Lagerkvist so beautifully captures in the following lines:

What is as deep as absence?
What fills my heart like emptiness?
What fills the soul like longing for something that does not exist,
Which it knows does not exist?

Others find peace in you.
Others burn in your fire, rest in your burning arms.
But what is their bliss
compared to my emptiness,
their glowing union with you
compared to my loneliness.

Maybe it is the same dark chamber of Being that the Austrian poet Rainer Maria Rilke alludes to in his first letter to Franz Xaver Kappus: "Therefore, my dear friend, I know of no other advice than this: Go within and scale the depths of your being from which your very life springs forth." Every poet has a landscape of language hidden in the recesses of his being. Most of them strive and slide into oblivion. However, there are a fortunate few, who get to that spring of language – that magic casement in the dark chamber of one's being. In the dark, most find themselves stranded on the threshold of words, some after countless knocks manage to get into the chamber; however, it is only a chosen few who get to open the casement and see that in the moonlit oblivion the first tribe of poetry is still waiting with the look of language in its eyes[5]. And all the false consolations of unclaimed and interpretable words have evaporated. There is only language and language, without beginning and without end. As the Swedish poet, Tomas Gosta Transtromer muses:

Tired of all who come with words, words but no language
I went to the snow-covered island.
The wild does not have words.
The unwritten pages spread themselves out in all
directions!
I come across the marks of roe-deer's hooves in the snow.
Language, but no words[6].

The grammar of feelings and the grammar of expression run contrary to one another. Maybe what is expressed is not how it was felt. This is, in fact, one of the reasons why most of the contemplative traditions emphasise silence. I, for one, believe that poetry should be meditated upon in silence, so that the meanings come out of their burrows unharmed. This is, in fact, one of the reasons behind my disinclination towards 'slam ~~poetry~~' (a monstrous practice. I won't call it poetry in the first place), '~~poetry~~ clubs', '~~literature~~ festivals', '~~creative~~ writing programmes and competitions' and other such modes of spirit-slaughtering. As Ruskin Bond writes in his autobiographical story, "Life with Father": "Some of us are born sensitive. And, if, on top of that, we are pulled about in different directions (both emotionally and physically), we might just end up becoming writers. No, we don't become writers in schools of creative writing. We become writers before we learn to write. The rest is simply learning how to put it all together." One must be patient with words so that they reveal themselves[7]. Maybe it is this element of wonder that V. S. Naipaul alludes to in his meditations on the craft of writing. There is nothing more tragic than inflicting interpretations on poetry with complete disregard for its spirit, which as Sri Aurobindo posits, remains unplumbed by the discursive intellect[8]. Poetry can defend itself. It does not need to be propped against other disciplines for any kind of desired redemption. If it cannot stand on its own unsupported, it need not stand at all.

However, such an approach to poetry in no way cancels out its social dimension; though it is my contention that poetry must thrive outside the realm of utility[9]. It should not just be a vehicle to carry other cargoes to their intended destination. It should be an end in itself by not committing itself to the humiliating existence in the shadows of other disciplines. Unlike some of the other modes of human understanding and being, that aim at some kind of an object of arrival by holding on to certain problems quite doggedly, poetry shows the direction to our state of perpetual homelessness – the ultimate human condition. And it is this state, which has turned me into a seeker to understand the undulating whispers of the mystery of human existence through successive seasons. As these lines from the *Iliad* whisper:

Like leaves on trees the race of man is found,
Now green in youth, now withering on the ground:
Another race the following spring supplies,
They fall successive, and successive rise;[10]

However, poetry for me is not a mirror that reflects life alone. It is, on the other hand, the still, dark and limpid waters of a pond reflecting the shadows of Being by further deepening its mystery. Poetry does not offer readymade answers to our *vrttis* (thought-waves), but leaves us with bouquets of questions. And if one pursues these questions, one may fall into the silences of one's Being. And here I offer you my questions contained in *A Letterbox Across Time.*

Bidyut Bhusan Jena
Bangalore

[1] My salutations to the progenitors of the universe – Mother Parvati (Parvati) and Lord Shiva (Parameshvara), who are indivisible like the Word (vAk) and its meaning (artha), for the attainment of the true understanding of the words and their meanings.
[2] The Brahman is without beginning or end, whose very essence is the word, who is the cause of the manifested phonemes, who appears as the objects, from whom the creation of the world proceeds. (1.Ch. 1, *Vakyapadiya*). Refer to K. A. Subramania Iyer's *The Vakyapadiya of Bhartrhari with the Vrtti* and *A History of Early Vedanta Philosophy, Part 2* by Hajime Nakamura.
[3] Something that walks hand-in-hand with us and contributes to out well-being. (a free translation)
[4] Read Steiner's celebrated book *After Babel: Aspects of Language and Translation.*
[5] As Albert Camus writes in the preface to his *Lyrical and Critical Essays*: "a man's work is nothing but this slow trek to rediscover, through the detours of art, those two or three great and simple images in whose presence his heart first opened. This is why, perhaps, after working and producing for twenty years, I still live with the idea that my work has not even begun."
[6] "From March '79". Translated by John F. Deane.
[7] Read Nissim Ezekiel's poem, "Poet, Lover, Birdwatcher".
[8] Read Sri Aurobindo's *The Future Poetry.* Also, read William James' reflection(s) on the "noetic" state(s).
[9] The other important dimension being *Ananda* (Bliss).
[10] Translated by Alexander Pope.

CONTENTS

No one behind, no one ahead.
The path the ancients cleared has closed.
And the other path, everyone's path,
easy and wide, goes nowhere.
I am alone and find my way.
—Dharmakirti

Beauty is not
in what the words say
but in that which they say without saying it:
not naked, but through a veil,
breasts become desirable.
—Vallana

(Adapted from classical Sanskrit by Octavio Paz)

The Bicycle

The bicycle still leans against the mossy wall under
the village end old asvattha, with deflated tyres,
rusted body, bent rims, lost spokes and silent bell.
It leans against the mossy wall half buried in sand.

I go there, when the day softens into dusk;
when the birds return to the asvattha with the day's dirge
on their tired wings that hide the residue of the conversation
between the paddy field and the farmer
whose son died from snakebite.

After the rain bathes the bicycle, the tender leaves of asvattha
play with it all day long with the frogs under its drip-drop.
Go there in summer and you'll see goats, dogs and cows rubbing
themselves against the bicycle and resting under the asvattha.

When crickets turn the nights into a prehistoric song,
the pages of the village's story book are turned.
The tyres inflate, the rims stand straight, the
spokes find their holes in the dark and the music
of the bell calls up songs of forgotten pyres.

Don't be in a hurry to pay it a visit, for the
bicycle will be there for many a season to come.
Except the wind, the sun, the rain, the tender leaves
of asvattha, frogs, goats, dogs, cows and the village bull,
no one else can ever touch it, for they say its owner has been
guarding it even years after he came under a stray truck.

Creation Myth

A separate sky is being woven for you
with a separate sun stitched to it;
a separate sea with
horizons on all its sides.

Just listen to me and wait on your
frozen boat for some more ages.

After all his world-wily ways,
a weary traveller is on his way
through the forest of this night
across which you wait on your
frozen boat on the cursed sea.

With the touch of his feet will
melt away the burden of your years;
and the ageing ice of your sea.

Believe me, for I have heard it all
in uninterrupted prophecies.

Moondrops

The other night the molten moon
dropped through the chinks in the thatch.

In another era,
mother had told him that
the moon was his uncle.

Years have elapsed since his uncle
was placed on pyre on a moonlit night, and
his mother did not return from across the river–
an undulating stretch, where the moon reigned
and the storm had withered the leaves of
of the old banyan, through which
he had seen the moon of that night.

While collecting the moondrops
in his cracked earthen pan,
he saw uncle in it for the first time,
and wished mother was there to see him too.

Too much thinking numbed his senses;
and the beggar fell asleep hungry,
with the pan of molten moon by his side.

A Place

Withered leaves still adorn
the pathway to the
moss-clothed abandoned house.

They say, the old priest still lights diyas
before the vermilion-smeared deity.

And somewhere across the paddy fields
the small river still flows by
with a half-remembered song.

And on moonlit nights still comes alive
the landscape of longing.

Across the Night

All roads fall into a pathway
that meanders through
the lush green paddy fields
leading to a mountain
that almost touches the sky.

On starry nights you could
climb up the mountain and
pluck stars.
But be careful,
the stars might wilt
in your hand if you
have not waited all your life.

You could consign the plucked stars
to the river across the mountain as
libation and sail into the silences
of the night on the boat
that has been waiting somewhere
on the banks of the river for ages.

But remember,
there is a region across the night
from where there is no return.

A Photograph

Those moments melted away like the
cubes of ice in a glass of Old Monk.

Like perfume in the air,
the smoke of their cigarettes was lost in the
ghazals of Mehdi Hassan that lay brooding
in the region between longing and loss.

And after the pitter-patter,
on the window was the residue
of the evening's rain.

Some moments are woven like memories.
Some friendships are preserved like pain.

Hampi – I

You must become Hampi
before you decide to visit it.
Or else it would elude you.

You may devour history books;
or listen to its stories from many a mouth,
yet Hampi would forever remain a mystery.

No one can tell you how to,
but you must become Hampi yourself.
Or just begin an unplanned journey to it,
and somewhere on the way you will become it.

You mustn't carry a road-map with you
or hire a competent guide.
Hampi will direct you to it
by whispering a time into your being –
a different order of time, which *Is*.

A Poet's Grave

While excavating the dried-up riverbed,
and the area around it,
they stumbled upon a grave.

In another time,
a man visited that place every evening
to engrave poems on the
waters of the river that rippled and whirled,
on the tired wings of the homeward birds,
on the trees that patterned the horizon
and on the gusts of wind that now and then
rustled the reeds along the riverbank.

One evening when the moon was up,
and the undulating whisper of bhajans
flitted from one gust of wind to another,
he offered the blank pages of his body
to the river while humming a song.

As they dug the grave deeper,
what they found was loose pages of poetry
separated by iridescent sand.

Bagha

Bagha was upset.

The garbage had been removed
and the place was clean and dry.

Next to what used to be
a heap of garbage – rich with leftovers of
dry and half eaten bread, semi-rotten
pieces of chicken, mutton and fish,
rotten vegetables, dead rats and all that,
now stood the life-size cut-out of some
local leader, clad in complete white.

Bagha, the mad beggar, was doubtful.

While digging into the crust
of dirt on his scalp with his
dark nails, he was thinking:
"Can this life-size cut-out calm
my hunger like the rich garbage-heap did?"

You–This Earth

As fog patterns the path
to the cremation ground,
you fall as water droplets
along the track of my vision,
now restless, now still like the
waters of the ancestral pond.

November, the month of
gnawing emptiness, teases the
rusted strings of one's being
by bringing you from across
the paddy fields of memory.

As the mango trees look on,
you escape the chanting of
the family priest and as waters
return to the eyes you had lent me
years ago.

And silently flows Kharasua with
the songs of this patch of land
where you all grow like trees.

Seeing

Carrying the baby inside,
the mother-cat walks the day.
But you can't see.

She knows the nests of the sparrows,
the shoal of fish under the limpid waters,
the baby mangoes falling into the pond and
the summer breeze in the bamboo clump.

But you can't see.

And when (the) night arrives hiding behind
the mango and tamarind trees,
she patiently sits on half-walls covered with
years of moss, looking at the moon.

But you can't see,
for you interpret;
and she doesn't.

Monku

The mother
kept on licking the
cold body of Monku,
that lay on the roadside,
the whole day.

She waited by its side
till the evening and then
left when it started to rain.

Amidst the downpour,
there was a little water
in the eyes of the cobbler's
five year old child.

"Monku, the puppy,
shouldn't have crossed
the road alone."

Madhu: In Memoriam

After working on it for days,
these civilized people
returned your body to me.

It was too cold and heavy
for my old arms.
You're not the child anymore.

But your body hid
another body in it –
alive, pregnant and hungry.

Now, they will visit us –
so many people for
the first time in our life.

They will visit us
with their machines
and machine-like words.

They might ask me,
how I feel after losing you.
They might shed tears too.

All of them will leave
after collecting material
for their stories.

They'll bury you once again
in newspapers, TV channels
and in their heads.

In a day or two everything
will die down, and the forest
will regain its primitive silence.

The forest sees it all
with its prehistoric eyes.
It is *aadim* – the timeless.

They call us *adivasis*.
We were before them all.
We will be after everything is gone.

Renunciation

You stood across the
rain of fourteen years.

Opening the door wide
you let me into your
dilapidated ancestral house.

Nothing much had changed.

The painting by Van Gogh
still adorned the cracked wall
next to the photograph of
your late parents.

The curls still played with
the mole under your right ear.
You still wore bindi of the
same colour and liked tea
with an extra spoon of sugar.

The rain and the pattern(s) of
our breathing assured me that
the years gone by in the scheme
of things meant nothing.

We were not the banks of
a boatless river after all.

After dinner when you offered
me as libation to the brooding rain,
from the corner of my eyes I
saw the used packets of insecurity
in your old trash can.

Ancestral Darkness

Akhaya Mohanty's
smruti tume paunsa talara nian
moistened his eyes.

The day was softening into evening
and the koels in the mango trees
signalling phaguna were silent.

With his father's old Philips radio
by his side, he was preparing for a
romantic Vividh Bharti night.

And the mango trees were being
engulfed by the flames of an
ancestral darkness.

The Intimate No-Longer

Your photograph is like a leaf,
seen through the limpid waters
of the village pond - immobile at
the bottom - the minnows' home.

And you cannot be touched
without disturbing this intimate
cold still crystal indifference.

What if you slide into an
irretrievable elsewhere
as my fingers disturb this
prehistoric stillness!?

How can I let a not-yet engulf
You – my intimate no-longer!

Your Skin

Ages of sighs lay silent
in the folds of your skin –
the dark ripples of time.

But that night all I could
scan was the surface.

Maybe that was all
I was capable of.

And there were the ripples
of oblivion in the glass
staring at us from the table
as the night snuggled up
in the region between us.

Train Journeys

The wind splashed the residue of your
thoughts on to my face soaking
the edges of my inchoate dreams.

And now on the soaked path of my dreams,
hand-in-hand and with measured steps,
walk Shravasti, Kapilsvastu, Kurukshetra,
Avadh, Hampi, Alexandria, Athens, Cambodia,
the Mayans and others,
leaving behind muddy footprints across
the outskirts of my dreams.

Maybe all train journeys are like this.
The recalcitrant wind thus jumbles up
our worlds leaving a trail of half-tones
and assorted smells behind.

If you don't have the courage to straddle
worlds, then the trick is to stay away from the
direction of the wind that blows past you and me.

Hands

The hands, with the dirt and
dust of paths on them,
arrive, quickening in you
the nausea of ages.
Time portals, they only open,
when coins are dropped into them.

Drop a coin and the door opens
into a forest of kalpavrkshas.
Choose a vrksha to sit under to
experience the hunger of yugas
amidst the heave of nagas.

Do not ever forget to carry a
coin in your pocket, for the hands
arrive unannounced from across time.

A Farewell

The words are all gone,
leaving behind a trail of echoes.
Under a layer of dust the sheets
wait for no season of language.

At the window of night I have bade
farewell to the last tribe of poetry.

After You

After we were spent,
you prepared to leave by collecting
the fragments of your insecurity.

The rum in the bottle was still now,
on the blades of the fan the cobwebs
were invisible and the afternoon
weighed heavy on the fringes of our vision,
where ages rose, fell and melted away.

And after you reclaimed the bindi that
stuck on to the wall flecked with promises,
I made my way to the kitchen.
But you offered to do the dishes.

And with a smile I
walked you down the stairs.

Those strands of hair
lay motionless on the pillow.
The sky was once again overcast.
The window was open.

The Night

After the storm,
darkness was all that was.
After two bottles of beer
my bladder was full.
And you were gone leaving behind
two empty bottles on the table.

After many a stumble,
I reached the bathroom and
it smelt of beer, urine and you.
You had forgotten to flush; and
there was no water when I flushed.

Maybe the storm had done the trick.
That night our urine had to coexist.

I got back to my bed hungry;
and the pillow smelt of you.

The night was too long.

aaj jane ki zid na karo

I wanted you to stay; but
you had all the excuses
well rehearsed to leave.
And the water in your cup
was just above the teabag.

Thus surreptitiously I poured
some more water into it.

And somewhere in the semi-lit
corner of the room the
tender afternoon played
aaj jane ki zid na karo.

Pages

The pages of the place
are dog-eared now.
They have not been
turned for ages.

Like the motionless sands
of your town, they wait for
no one's return.

They soak in the moonlight;
take in the whispers of
the brooding afternoons.

And at the dead of night
the words slip through the
porous pages and fall into
each other's silences.

Nobody turns the pages,
for there is no meaning in them.
They are just pages -
dog-eared, yellow, porous.

Two Solitudes

I don't want to talk to you.

But wait for me where the tree still stands;
where the squirrels still play;
where the day softens into evening
and brings birds from another sky,
under which the ashes of the dead still lie.

Wait for me alone with your silence; and
with my share of silence I am on my way.

Perspiring Words

On that night of winter, your
perspiring words had travelled
all the way through my skin
into the soil of my being.

These days at the dead of night
I hear the chirping of birds hidden
behind the leaves of the trees within me.

And the leaves of these trees are moist,
like those words of that night of winter.

Arrival

There are days when
everything seems to come alive
with the intimations of
someone's arrival.

And as the day ripens into dusk,
someone patterns the
wilting edges of gulmohar with
the longings of ages past.

On days like these
one feels one has
always been a vagrant lover
without ever being in love.

Paws

A stray kitten is asleep
under the betel stall on the pavement
with the afternoon sun on its body,
where a little life still pulsates.

As you move a bit closer it
does not wake up – the little one,
but sleeps with the dust of the
streets on its fur and charcoal
of the vendors' stores on its nose.

After its mother came under
the wheels the other day,
the little one has run and run
first in search of its mother
and then in hunger all day.

Is this the age to find food for oneself?

As you run your fingers
through its fur, it wakes up with
the half open eyes of a baby

and again falls asleep with
your finger in its tender mouth.

And as you take its tender paws
in your hand, you remember how
years ago such a little one
had been caught red-handed while
trying to open the almirah
that contained fish, milk and sweets.

Such a little one too loved
the warmth of your lap in winter.

Notes

On moonlit nights,
the sea brings from unknown shores
the residue of the whispers of the nights –
words that observe you from behind the trees
on the beach that converse with each other
at the dead of night.

On moonless nights,
the sea hums for no one
the unrhymed songs of the ones,
who have spent on the shores alone
the sunsets of their life.

A Cone of Memory

The chickpea seller,
a boy of fourteen,
tore a page from
the battered book
to make a cone
for the next customer.

And on it he saw
the poem he had read
in his village school.

Pen-stand

The old pen-stand
leaned against the wall
with unused pens,
rusted scissors, bookmarks,
dust, spiderwebs, ants and
dead mosquitoes.

It also contained the
residue of our conversation
moistened by last year's rain.

Kashi Ghats

On the ghats of Kashi,
time is placed on pyres.

In the silences of the night
the unanchored boats are
ever-ready to take the
bodyless ones across the
frontiers of dukkha.

When you visit Kashi,
carry your pyre within.

Wait for your turn,
place your death of ages
on it and live.

And listen,
you will be ferried across
for free.

The Would-have-beens

Look at the crows
on the telephone cable
held by the entanglement of
wires from different houses.

The wires that have so
intricately woven a web,
do not interpret the birds
that sit on them.

When rains pattern them
with beads that hang still
like the residue of time,
I see you from the window.

Now I know without
interpreting the look of
Aschenbach at the sunset
of longing and

see how the Tadzio
I could not be in the Venice
that your look had inaugurated
on that evening of summer.

The Rainrise

You know, it rained today.
I pushed the curtain to
one side of the window after
almost a lifetime to see the rain.

It had frosted the window,
patterned the telephone cable
with beads and had seeped
under the carpet of asphalt
to let the soil exhale a smell
that was not unfamiliar.

As I opened the window,
letting the drops rest on my books,
notebooks, fountain pen and
study table, a smell from
another era crept into my being.

Do you remember
how we used to welcome the rain
into our small room through the window
with the Krushnachura almost

benignly sending out its bud-studded
tender branches into our world?

Years have elapsed since then –
the room, the window,
the Krushnachura,
the city and you.

But still in another city
the rain rises with the same
ache in the heart.

Rain is an ache after all!

The Curve

That afternoon
I ran after the bus
to have a glimpse of you
for the final time.

And then the road bent
after the cremation ground.

An Elegy

There is an elegy,
hidden somewhere under
the moss that covers
the walls of a city
to which one would
never return.

The Storm

And then rose the storm
clearing the trees and bushes off
dead leaves, flowers and nests.

Then after the first shower
he opened his window.
And the room was filled with
the smell of death.

Punctuation Marks

The full-stops that
he had buried have
sprouted semicolons.

Now the page of
his life awaits a
paragraph without
conclusion.

And on moonless nights
boats leave the semicolons
towards no shore.

The Burnt Petals

After the feast
the beasts once again
donned their skin and left.

And the next morning
a butterfly was struggling
to sit on the burnt petals
of a blood-smeared flower.

A Summer Tale

The heat of May tires
the vagrant girl carrying
those long pens to sell.

She falls asleep hungry on
the steps of the urine-soaked
dilapidated building.

In its shadowy corner
they cuddle the season
oblivious to curious eyes.

Bricks

The bricks carrying
the initials of the owner
lie intact inside the tomb
on the outskirts of the town.

The tropical climate has
disfigured the name and
years of the dead.

Scented Streets

On winter afternoons,
these streets wear a
look of departure and
smell of longing.

Melting

You are like a bottle
of coconut oil in winter.
The sunlight of memory
is all I need to melt you.

And then, from my palm
you are all over my body.

A Lost Night

After you left, the evening
turned cold like a corpse.

As the fog of ages gathered
over the horizon across
the paddy fields, I suspended
the moment by removing
battery from the wall clock.

And on the pillows were
dead mosquitoes –
the souvenirs of a night lost.

Embers

You lay immobile like a
track through paddy fields
with dew on the wild grass
patterning its sides.

In your hair of night
I saw the embers of
an unrehearsed time.

The Letterbox

Time smuggled you out of
my world and dropped into
the letterbox across ages.

And then, I,
an archive of your memories,
offered myself as libation
to the dust of years.

A Chase

You didn't leave any address.
But after the first shower,
I saw glimpses of you,
now here, now gone in the
drops that chased each other
on the windowpane.

A Cycle

Leaves fell unheard,
unnoticed in the forest of
a time lost.

After the siesta, when
you came to my room,
I saw around your eyes
the locked doors of the
secret tunnel to the forest.

In my teacup I saw those
glimpses, and you, with
the residue of the smile
of a bygone age in your eyes,
took me to the secret chamber
and made me open the doors
to the mouth of the tunnel
patterned by pubescent grass.

Then you took me into it
as I remembered the ages
once rehearsed and lost.

The Last Look

I saw you where the road bent,
hiding the Krushnachura,
making the cyclist disappear,
the road bent.

And when I saw you,
I felt as though I had opened
an envelope containing
a long awaited letter
from a place to which
I would never return.

I saw you where the road bent;
you vanished where the road bent.

Maybe

I won't dial your number anymore;
nor can I delete it from my phone.
New Years and Teachers' Days
will come and go silently, but
I won't dial your number anymore;
nor can I delete it from my phone.

How I wish I knew I was
seeing you for the final time
in an unrehearsed city, which, for
those moments, we had made our own –
you made everything your own –
people, places, moments and cancer!
The art came to you so naturally!
You were from a species long gone!

But, I will search for you elsewhere –
in the city of our beginnings –
one with those flecked walls,
where many an afternoon was made in a
room where maybe echoes reign now.

Maybe one day I'll dial your number again,
knowing that I won't find you at the other end.
Maybe one day I'll visit the city again
for those roads you and I had once walked.

Maybe I'll dial your number again
with the hope of hearing my nick name
uttered by a voice that I will hear no more!

A Routine

The birds on the electric wires
flew away as the garbage vehicle honked.
The neighbouring door opened, and
down the stairs the jingle of anklets.

Notes on a Sunset

The sun still hid behind
the undulating row of trees;
and the birds returned
with the note of the
day's death on their
tired wings.

Sitting on the
broken wooden bridge,
he had seen it all.
all these years.

And he knew,
one day the birds will return
with the day's dirge
on their tired wings to the
trees that hid the sun

in his absence!

A Painting

And yet another day.

I come to the bedroom
and see how like yesterday,
the afternoon sun has
painted the corner with
something like a poem;
something like a stare.

Maybe sun, afternoon, dust
and a corner is all one needs.

And then poetry is easy.

But are you empty enough
to store the echoes of the
waning day in some dusty
corner of your being, where
the sun visits every afternoon?

A Letter

In your town time walks
like an unblinking
pregnant cow.

The hospital, where
years ago they had
declared you a thing,
is now a municipality
corporation building.

But the chickpea seller
still sits next to the
Shiva temple.

They say he
doesn't pray anymore.

Unspent

Those afternoons
lie unspent in the
crevices of your city.

And all they need is some
warmth and moisture to
sprout like saplings from
the cracks of abandoned
buildings in the silences
of unrehearsed nights.

A Ritual

You are the wish for
which I still drop coins
into unknown rivers
from running trains.

A Supplication

Would you mind returning
the burden of those years
that I had forgotten in the
alleys of your body?

Was It All Real?

The moonlit oblivion
brought your face to me
through the limpid waters
of the pond of night.

And the dream broke
in ripples as my fingers
touched the still surface.

A shaft of moonlight had
entered the room and
sat staring at me from
the ancestral writing desk.

After the Pyre

On the municipality
toilet wall I saw an
inaccurate sketch
of you below your
phone number.

After years, finally,
the unfamiliar road
held out milestones.

And in the evening,
when I dialled your
number, I heard at
the other end, your
faltering voice through
a shared panting.

A Prophecy

On the pavements
across the urine alley
sits a bustling bazaar
of blessings under a
row of Kalpabrkshyas.

Just carry some coins with
you and choose one of the
hands that reach you from
the invisible corners of time.

Believe me, they will take
you to the frontiers of
the land of dreams.

Repetition

Like baby mangoes,
my dreams fell into
the village pond and
were found no more.

Years later, I saw father
looking at the mango
trees around the pond,
from his wheelchair.

And father's eyes were
as deep as the mute
waters of the pond with
some prophecy long
awaiting its turn.

Worlds

After the rain,
he took the moon out
of his cupboard and
stuck it into the holder
hanging from the clouds.

And next to the garbage heap
under the flyover, the beggar
and his dog resumed their
search for leftovers.

In the nearby township,
where lifts go up to the moon,
they were busy sipping
their jazz of dreams.

A Legend

On the banks of Kharasua,
stories run back to their holes
like crabs and hide upon
seeing you.

Through the holes they
disappear into a world below
to archive the destinies of
this patch of land.

How hard you may try,
you cannot lure them out
of those holes.

But you may like to wait for
that time of the day, when
Kharasua runs still, and sit on
one of its banks like the reeds,
the grass, the tired wind and them.

And then, they will come out of
the holes, look at you with their
eyes of time and take you to
the world below, from where
there is no return.

www.ingramcontent.com/pod-product-compliance
Lightning Source LLC
LaVergne TN
LVHW091617170726
843492LV00007B/2467

* 9 7 8 8 1 9 4 5 2 7 3 4 3 *